M000118079

MY TENDER LOVING SELF-CARE JOURNAL

THE WORKBOOK THAT MAKES SELF-CARE EASY

MANDY KUBICEK

Glad Panda Press
Omaha, Nebraska

Copyright © 2020 by Mandy Kubicek.

All rights reserved. No part of this publication may be reproduced, distributed or transmitted in any form or by any means, including photocopying, recording, or other electronic or mechanical methods, without the prior written permission of the publisher, except in the case of brief quotations embodied in critical reviews and certain other noncommercial uses permitted by copyright law. For permission requests, write to the publisher.

Glad Panda Press, Omaha, Nebraska

www.coachkubicek.com

My Tender Loving Self-Care Journal: The Workbook that Makes Self-Care Easy/Mandy Kubicek. —1st ed.

ISBN 978-1-7362854-0-4

Cover design by Teruko Tsubaki

Cover photography by PV productions

Author photo by Kimberly Dovi Photography

Remember

Wise words I want to remember:

CONTENTS

INTRODUCTION

Tender loving self-care

Which do you feel more often: exhausted or energized?
Impatient or peaceful?
Depressed or delighted?

What if you could consistently feel your best without emptying your retirement account or making a radical life change?

You can. The key is to consistently prioritize tender loving self-care.

Self-care is a practice of preserving or improving one's own health and wellbeing. It consists of the things we do and don't do to nourish, refuel, and feel our best. Yes, it can be getting the token massage. It can also be as simple as drinking water or as challenging as learning a foreign language. It can be something we do ourselves or it can involve asking for help, such as sharing a hug with a friend or hiring a therapist.

While self-care is nourishing by definition, it might not always be fun. For example, I dislike the sensation of flossing my teeth. Some of my molars are so tightly spaced that most flosses shred to pieces in my mouth. Yet I tend to floss every night because the satisfaction of doing so and avoiding another cavity outweighs my short-term discomfort. When taken as a whole, flossing nightly nourishes me. You may find that some of the activities that refuel you aren't all that pleasant in the moment. In this case, when you consider the practice as a whole, notice where it falls on the energy scale: more draining or more filling?

Though it might not always feel like fun, self-care is not draining.

As such, tender loving self-care requires a mental shift away from self-pressure toward compassion, which includes a supportive inner dialogue. We've all beaten ourselves up. We've said things to ourselves that we'd never say aloud to a friend.

When you fall short of your self-care expectations and the habitual self-attack kicks in, practice noticing and approaching the situation with curiosity instead of judgment. Why did you set the goal? Do you still want it? If so, what might help you move forward?

Finally, self-care is nothing new. It's something you've been doing your whole adult life, from eating when you're hungry to sleeping at night. **Tender loving self-care is simply an all-in approach you can choose to take to maximize your joy.**

Luckily, you already have everything you need. You've developed tools, habits, and beliefs that help you navigate the ups and downs of life. Are you aware of what these are? Are they easy for you to access on both your best and worst days?

This workbook will help you readily access that wisdom. Think of it as your personalized self-care game plan. By offering the space and structure to add your own insights alongside the provided stories and suggestions, it will help you easily prioritize your wellbeing no matter what stands in your way.

How to use this book

TL;DR Use this book in whatever way feels easy and fun.

At the beginning of this workbook, you'll find a quick-reference *Reminder* page. This is for capturing your favorite insights, quotes, and whatever else brings you joy.

This *Introduction* section provides key definitions, background information, and intention-setting questions to prepare you for what's to come.

In *Part 1: Ideate*, you'll find ideas for self-care activities plus ample space to add your own. As you read through the ideas, mark them up. You might circle ones that intrigue you, scribble out what's not for you, and fill in details. Add your own ideas with a list, a mind map, or drawings. Refer back to these pages to help you decide what action to take, especially when you're not feeling your best.

Part 2: Commit provides pages to record your personal commitments related to self-care. Use it to set effective goals and reflect on your experiences.

Finally, *Part 3: Write* includes journaling prompts to help you relieve stress, feel more joyful, make clear decisions, and take action. Use these questions and the blank journaling pages that follow at any time to connect with your own creativity and wisdom about what you need. Consider adding newfound insights, activity ideas, and goals to the earlier sections of this book for quick reference.

Remember: Tender loving self-care doesn't feel like another obligation. To be truly nourished, let the journey be easy and fun.

Background

Though everything in this book is bite-sized, it will prepare you to make life changes that are so big you can't even envision them yet.

As a Certified Life Coach, I help people find and move into more meaningful careers. Their first steps aren't what you might expect. We don't talk about their strengths, study the job market, or analyze their current career options. Instead, we almost always start with the types of things you'll find in this workbook.

Why?

Change is hard. To gather the energy we need to make a sustainable transformation, we often have to begin by investing in our relationship with ourselves. As with any intimate long-term relationship, we have to listen, gradually build trust by acting on what we hear, demonstrate our love, and accept the love that's offered.

Personally, my biggest challenge in this all-important partnership is the listening part. I tend to avoid slowing down enough to feel my full range of emotions. I can trace this discomfort avoidance all the way back to a traumatic experience when I was just seven years old.

My mom woke my dad early that Christmas Eve complaining of a severe headache, one more excruciating than any migraine she'd ever experienced. In the hospital, we learned that she had a ruptured brain aneurysm. When I visited my bedridden mom shortly before the term brain-dead entered my second-grade vocabulary, it wasn't exactly her I saw. During one visit, I took the new Crimp 'n Curl Cabbage Patch doll that she had bought, wrapped, and placed under the tree for me.

"What a beautiful doll!" she said. "Where did you get it?" My stomach sank upon hearing the distance between us that had never been there before.

After two weeks in the hospital mentally time traveling and undergoing multiple brain surgeries, my thirty-five-year-old mother died. I was so ill-equipped for this loss that my grief turned into suicidal ideation by early adolescence. That faded into a mild recurring depression that turned acute in my late twenties, when I found myself bedbound by the weight of my despair— sometimes for days at a time.

I survived and eventually thrived. I tried many things to feel better. I took antidepressants, saw therapists, looked for meaning by volunteering with grieving kids, changed jobs, exercised, prayed, and read countless self-help books. Some things helped more than others. A five-year therapy relationship brought me more lasting peace than I had ever remembered experiencing. She helped me overcome trauma while teaching me the emotional skills that my self-care practices had been lacking. From there I discovered coaching, in which I found both a fulfilling career and a powerful toolset I continue to use daily to improve my own life.

In general, I'm more joyful than ever before. Even so, three decades after that early traumatic loss and years since I've spent a day in bed depressed, diligently prioritizing my wellbeing hasn't stopped being important.

For me, tender loving self-care includes things like fitness plans made more fun by training for challenging races, a delightful morning routine with loose-leaf tea and absolute quiet, and being myself by sparking laughter that lightens heavy conversations. It includes many of the ideas you'll read in this book, delivered in varying doses at varying times, following the guidance of my body, mind, heart, and soul as best as I can in each moment.

I wrote this book, in part, because it helps me prioritize tender loving self-care.

I hope it helps you, too.

Let's get started

Answer these questions to set yourself up for self-care success.

What does tender loving self-care mean to me?

Why do I want to take tender loving care of myself?

What might get in the way of me taking tender loving care of myself?

What do I need to overcome these challenges?

PART 1: IDEATE

ACTIVITY IDEAS

Tips

The following pages include a variety of categorized self-care activity ideas. Scattered among the idea lists are brief stories that give honest, real-world perspectives of self-care in action.

As you read through the ideas, mark them up. You might circle ones that intrigue you, scribble out what's not for you, and fill in details. Add your own ideas with a list, a mind map, or drawings. At the end of the section is additional space to capture your favorite ideas, if that's useful.

You can refer back to these pages to help you decide what action to take, especially when you're not feeling your best.

Underwater

I lay awake in bed, the comforter tucked up to my neck, and squinted my eyes against the midday sun that peeked around the edges of our bedroom shades. For no obvious reason, I felt intensely sad. My mind spun with negative thoughts about my inadequacies. My body felt immovable and I barely breathed, as if a powerful undertow had pulled me underwater.

My husband curled behind me on top of the covers. "You could take a bath," he offered gently, suggesting an activity he had seen soothe me countless times before.

I responded by not responding.

Our emotional state affects our ability to creatively solve problems. This is why, on a tough day like that one, I simply had no idea what I might enjoy. When I'm struggling, my husband is of great support. So are my lists.

I keep a document that lists evidence to remind me that I'm a good coach: testimonials, client results, and joyous words muttered aloud at the end of a transformational coaching session.

The bulletin board in my home office displays nine images I found online to represent *My Crew*: the archetypal personalities within me who are always available to help. *The Engineer* thumbs her cell phone, *The Rebel* dons a sexy undercut, and *The Magical Child* grins in her unicorn headband and tutu.

I tag complimentary emails with the label *warm fuzzies*.

I keep a list of one-minute mood boosters: actions that can quickly lift me out of a funk, slightly if not completely, in sixty seconds or less.

The unpredictable waves of painful emotions will come again. They always do. Why not load yourself up with life preservers?

1-minute mood boosters

Which of these ideas might work for me?

- Write a haiku about what's upsetting me (5, 7, 5 syllables)
- Come up with a plan to do one kind thing for someone else soon
- Lift my chin, close my eyes, grin a wide cheesy smile, and hold it for a few breaths
- Drink a glass of water
- Listen to an upbeat song, like:
- Move (jump, do a handstand, hula hoop)
- Look at pictures or videos of people I love
- Recall an amazing memory, for example:
- Tell myself one thing I'm good at while taking 4 deep breaths
- Step outside

How else can I quickly boost my mood—say, in one minute
or less?

Community

Which of these ideas do I like?

- Text a joke or compliment to a friend
- Attend a religious service
- Think about a loved one and what I appreciate about them
- Ask for help
- Write a snail-mail letter to thank someone who has impacted my life
- Join a club
- Take a break from social media
- Eat a meal with a good friend
- Forgive someone
- Find a future event to attend and add it to my calendar

How else would I like to connect with others?

Distracted

A coach once asked me, "What do you need?"

To slow down, I immediately thought. The words felt clear and peaceful. Without even trying to do so, I relaxed into my chair and took a deep breath.

Then, so quickly that I could have completely missed my initial response, I had a flurry of different thoughts. *That's a bad idea. That's not what I want. I have too many important goals to slow down!* These beliefs felt chaotic, as if a crowd of stressed-out Black-Friday shoppers were sprinting through my head filling their massive carts with discounted garbage. My heart sped up while my neck and shoulders squeezed upward.

My initial insight was unbearably uncomfortable. It went against the norms of my culture. Slow down? Achieve less? Isn't that the exact opposite of what I'm supposed to value?

I was terrified by the idea of slowing down.

With practice, I've come to recognize that the thoughts that make me feel calm and steady are always wiser than the frantic ones that cause me physical tension. We all have this straightforward and powerful voice of inner wisdom, but it can be difficult to hear. Fear is louder.

In the face of this fear, we tend to self-soothe with distractions that temporarily quiet all of the voices. I distract myself by consuming back-to-back TV shows, sugary foods, and depressing news. I escape inside the pages of fictional worlds. And my hands-down favorite distraction: I consume never-ending work projects.

When I do listen, I always find that it's not as dangerous as it had seemed. Whatever the calm, steady voice suggests is a good type of scary: a clear path toward what I truly desire.

What are your go-to methods of distraction? What might be possible if, instead, you listened?

Consumption

Which of these ideas interest me?

- Read an uplifting email newsletter
- Eat an unhealthy meal or snack that I love, without guilt
- Display photos of my biggest fans
- Buy something I want
- Instead of buying something I want, write it down and wait at least one week before purchasing
- Pick one healthful food at a time and make consuming it a daily habit
- Turn off digital notifications
- Get rid of three items in my home, car, or office that I don't need nor want
- Mindfully eat a meal, focusing my attention on the food and doing nothing else
- Have a screen-free day (unplug from TV, the Internet, and all other screens)

How else can I feel my best through what I consume, from food to information?

Playful

I found inspiration in a young pop star on *Carpool Karaoke*.

One evening, after giggling along with *The Office* bloopers on YouTube, I found Rainn Wilson interviewing Billie Eilish, some pop star I hadn't heard of. I quickly learned three things: Billie was wildly famous, I liked her song *Bad Guy*, and her story of success was fascinating.

This interview snippet demonstrates why I fell in love with her story.

"Isn't that crazy?" James Corden says, referring to her first hit song *Ocean Eyes*, which she recorded at a young age with her brother. "Something you do at thirteen kick starts..."

"Something I do for, like, no reason besides the fact that it was just for fun."

She was being a kid, staying up late to play with her big brother. And millions of her fans would have missed out if she hadn't devoted her free time to her unique interpretation of fun. Her story inspires me to reflect on what I do and, more honestly, what I choose *not* to do.

Many of us feel less and less playful as we grow up. Without us noticing this root cause, we become bored, exhausted, or hopelessly without meaning. This doesn't seem like an accident. Our culture glorifies work. When play is exalted, it's portrayed as a consumerist's hobby requiring expensive electronics, day spa appointments, or international vacations, instead of what it is: an approach to life that's always available to us. And creativity, perhaps the epitome of play, is seen as a unique trait reserved for the select few.

But all humans are creative, and we all benefit from an integration of both work and play.

The good news is that we don't have to be children to engage with the world through a child's point of view. We can play at any age, whether it's with paper airplanes and basketballs or more grown-up toys like fancy cookware and free time on our calendars.

When was the last time you felt playful? What creative project would you like to pursue just for fun?

Having fun is, in itself, worthwhile. Plus, who knows what creative brilliance you might birth.

Creativity

Which ideas sound enjoyable?

- Make one small improvement to an area of my home to make it more beautiful, calming, cozy, or joyful
- Play a musical instrument, for example:
- Arrange flowers in a vase
- Wear clothes I love, combined and styled in a new way
- Do an art project designed for kids
- Plan a party
- Take cell-phone photos of nature
- Invent and build a new board game
- Cook a meal or prepare a snack, then plate it beautifully
- Design and create greeting cards

What else could I create just for fun?

Lighter

At the starting line, I was so excited that I couldn't stop smiling. After months of training, I was ready to run my first race. I hopped left to right, jittery with nerves, wondering if I had time to hit the porta-potty one more time. Meanwhile, the edges of my awareness remained occupied by my brother, Aaron.

A few days prior, I received a devastating call from my sister-in-law: Aaron had died in a motorcycle accident on his way to work.

I could have skipped the race. There would always be another 5K. But after three days of sobbing at home, I needed the distraction.

The race official announced the start, and I passed under the sign at my carefully-planned pace. I trotted along the quiet Nebraska highway, nestled between green grass and forest, listening to the satisfying clap-clap of rubber soles on concrete. As the crowd of runners around me thinned, I began to ruminate on how much I missed my brother. I seethed, *Why did he have to die?* I balled my hands into fists and pumped my arms harder.

Anger had been coming over me in waves since that phone call. At home, sitting alone on the deck or curled up with an afghan on the couch, the tension had stayed lodged in my chest and shoulders, stuck as relentlessly as gum in hair.

While running, though, the anger felt different. It pulsed throughout my body, down my arms and hands and out, as if dripping from my fingertips. It moved through my torso, down my strong legs, and out of the bottom of my feet, left behind to evaporate on the hot concrete. As I expressed my feelings in this physical and private way, I began to feel lighter.

The crowd clapped and cheered as I raced under the *Finish* sign, beaming with pride.

Strangely, even though my body was exhausted, I felt energized. In anger's place was a new and comforting warmth telling me that everything was as it should be.

What feelings remain in your body waiting to be expressed? What would help them move through you?

Expression

Which of these ideas might work for me?

- When grieving a death, do something that makes me think of fond memories of the person
- Use a mantra to help me remember that I will be okay and only need to handle this very moment, for example, *I am here now* or:
- Do a slow body scan: notice any physical sensations from my toes to the top of my head
- When I feel an unpleasant emotion, mentally thank the sensation for existing and for communicating with me
- Journal about what happened and how I feel about it
- Take a break from feeling my uncomfortable feelings (watch TV, sleep, have fun)
- Go for a walk, run, or bike ride
- Tell my story to a trusted person
- Draw my feelings
- Do what feels good (laugh, cry, scream)

How else can I allow and express my uncomfortable emotional experiences?

Gratitude

Which of these ideas do I like?

- Make eye contact and thank the grocery clerk or barista
- Before eating dinner with my family, take turns sharing aloud what we're grateful for from the day
- When something lousy happens, consider the opposite: *How is this wonderful?*
- Find an inspiring quote about gratitude and record it in the front of this book
- Remember that I could, at any time, lose the people and things I love most
- Pick a specific joyful memory and write about it in detail
- Stand naked in front of the bathroom mirror, admire my miraculous body, and thank it for everything it has given me
- In the next email I write, genuinely compliment the recipient
- Keep a nightly gratitude journal and before bed, write a few specific phrases about things I was grateful for from that day
- Make a list of things I love about myself

How else might I consistently appreciate the goodness in
my life?

Flabbergasted

Feeling unclear about what actions count as self-care?

Consider this funny true story which illustrates what self-care *is* and *is not*.

Examples of self-care are underlined.

Example

I once <u>bought myself a beautiful stone-shaped pedometer</u>. <u>Delighted to see my steps increase</u>, I started <u>walking and running more</u>.

One day, the gorgeous device fell from the waist of my pants into the toilet. Worried about its replacement cost, I carefully disinfected its porous surface. It seemed safe, and yet, was that a stain on one corner?

Several days later, prompted by my flabbergasted husband's wise words, I <u>threw the pedometer away</u>.

Humor

What makes me laugh?

- Ask a talkative toddler to explain something to me
- When autocorrect fails, send my text anyway so we can both laugh at it
- Collect and play with toys, such as:
- Get together with family and retell funny family history stories
- Use a novelty pen
- Hang out with people who laugh often and make me laugh
- Listen to a funny podcast, for example:
- Tell someone about an embarrassing moment I had
- Go to my favorite online source(s) of humor, like:
- Fake laugh

How else can I laugh a little more every day?

Indulgence

What brings me pleasure?

- Go for a drive through the countryside with the windows down
- Listen to the sound of rain using the website <u>rain.today</u>
- Put on an outfit I love
- Make fresh-squeezed fruit juice
- While at work, take a break to read fiction
- Light a candle or build a fire
- Relax in or near a pool
- Snuggle with a blanket and/or a loved one
- Use a heated rice bag against my body
- Visit a beautiful place, like:

What else delights my senses of sight, sound, smell, taste, and touch?

Boosted

One humid morning, I was slowly running up a steep hill on a quiet block of downtown Omaha. I was determined not to quit despite the burning in my legs and the voice in my head urging me to do so. A man I was passing made eye contact, smiled, and gave me a thumbs up. I smiled back and found myself effortlessly accelerating with a boost of newfound confidence.

Years later, I still remember that moment and his tiny act of kindness.

What memories will you create?

Kindness

What could I do for someone else?

- Listen to someone without interrupting, sharing, or trying to solve their problem
- Go for a walk, picking up litter and pet waste
- Tell the truth
- Give a generous tip at the coffee shop
- Reach out to someone months after their trauma and offer specific support
- Volunteer, for example:
- Hold a door open
- After a snowfall, shovel someone else's driveway
- Make a monetary or in-kind donation
- Keep conversations positive by not complaining or criticizing

How else would I like to show my kindness and generosity?

Mastery

What skills do I enjoy using?

- Assemble a jigsaw puzzle
- Cook or bake
- Teach my pet a new trick
- Identify an easy next step toward my most ambitious dream and complete it
- Study a foreign language, for example with the *Duolingo* app
- Reconstruct an iconic building with a construction toy such as Legos
- Read a book that teaches me about the experience of people different from myself
- Explore my genealogy
- Solve a Rubik's cube
- Finish an incomplete project

What else might be energizing to learn or accomplish?

Awkward

Sometimes I use the Pomodoro Technique. I set a timer for twenty-five minutes, focus on a task, then take a five-minute break before focusing for another twenty-five.

The other day when my break time hit, I quickly turned off the alarm. Before I could plan how to spend those delightful five minutes, I realized that I had left my home office and was standing over my kitchen counter, AirPods in, thumbing to my *Dancy Chill* Spotify playlist. It's like my body carried me there, fully aware of what it needed and communicating as efficiently as possible in that rare moment of mental quietude.

Then, I danced.

Take whatever you're picturing and add a boatload of middle-school-dance awkwardness. But also fill me with pure joy. It felt unbelievably satisfying to just move and sing without caring how I might be perceived.

Movement and breath are so valuable, especially in times of crisis and grief. Our emotions exist in our bodies and need to be expressed. What did my dancing have to do with my emotional state that day? I don't know.

And I don't have to know—that's the point.

Stand up right now and shake. Shake an arm, then the other. Lift a leg and shake your foot. Jump up a few times. Stretch your mouth. Laugh.

Keep letting your brilliant body move you.

Movement

What type of movement does my body crave?

- Take a nap or go to sleep
- Go for a walk, run, or bike ride outside
- Do yard work
- Wake up naturally without an alarm clock
- Declutter one category of items in my home (such as pants or books)
- Stretch
- Play fetch with a dog
- Play a sport with others
- Complete a household chore, repair, or project for someone else
- Do bodyweight exercises

What other forms of exercise do I enjoy?

Nature

Which of these ideas interest me?

- Care for a houseplant
- Buy locally-grown produce
- Walk outside while noticing one sense at a time (*What do I hear? What do I smell?*)
- Visit a nearby forest, body of water, or botanical garden
- Use nature-inspired scents indoors
- Sit on a park bench and listen to the sounds of nature
- Put a picture of nature where I'll see it often (desktop background, cell phone lock screen, the fridge)
- Look out a window
- Garden
- Walk in the grass barefoot

How else can I allow nature to nourish me?

Here

I watch my dog's brindle back rise and fall with the steady rhythm of her breath. Her body is spread across a patch of sunlight that has warmed the wood floor of our living room. Beyond two half-open eyes, her snout—now dusted at the edges with white—rests between two outstretched paws. Her floppy ears perk at the sound of a truck passing by. As the truck quiets, I notice that birds are chirping just outside of our open windows.

Even though I'm perfectly safe here on the couch on this idyllic spring day, my body is rigid with allover anxiety.

Have you ever noticed how quickly we humans can create pure terror out of thin air?

It's impressive, even if unproductive in most modern scenarios. I don't know this particular anxiety's source exactly, but I've stopped analyzing. I find it more useful to let it be without judgment.

This is why I'm sitting here doing nothing but noticing the sensory details of my immediate surroundings. I breathe and observe. Again and again I pull myself out of an imagined future or a regretted past, back into this moment.

I watch green trees sway in the distance. The dog sits up now, her nails clicking as she repositions. She stares at me as if to say, "Can't you see that sunshine? Let's go outside! Let's play, Mom!"

I blink back a tear, suddenly overtaken with gratitude.

Take a moment right now to notice your immediate surroundings. What time is it? Where are you? What do you see, hear, and smell? What textures do you feel against your skin? Turn your attention to the insides of your body and notice what's happening there, too.

Notice how being here now changes your experience.

Nothingness

Which of these do I want to try?

- Sit on the couch and do nothing

- Go to bed early

- Sit in silence with my eyes closed and simply hear every sound (near and far, loud and subtle) without analyzing its likely source

- Walk slowly around my neighborhood, noticing and mentally naming everything I see (sidewalk, crack, leaf, person, hat, vehicle, hood, dent...)

- Doodle or color

- Listen to a guided meditation, such as:

- While sipping my morning drink, notice the beauty in its aroma, temperature, taste, texture, and color

- Lay on the floor with my pet

- Sit on the deck and watch the sky

- When I find myself resisting doing nothing, journal about it: *What am I afraid of?*

How else can I practice quieting my mind, resting my body, doing nothing?

Right

I stood at the sink examining each individual blackberry for signs of fuzzy white mold. After tossing half of the berries into the trash, I rinsed what was left in the strainer in the sink. Then I scooted a stool up to the kitchen counter with my disappointing breakfast.

He didn't even check for mold, I thought as I inhaled the finger-staining food. My husband had bought the high-priced berries, my favorite fruit, just two days prior. *He doesn't give a damn about my food.*

When I heard Bob's alarm thirty minutes or so later, I hustled to our bedroom.

"Good morning!" I sang, feigning affection though my jaw was still tight with frustration.

"Morning," Bob mumbled.

"I had to throw away the blackberries." Part of me was impatient to point out what he had done wrong. Another part of me watched helplessly as I carried out this compulsion.

"I looked," he defended, not with righteousness but with what seemed like empathetic disappointment. "I didn't see any mold."

"I know," I replied as if I wasn't blaming him. "Most of it was inside." I was back-peddling, faking non-judgment with my words in that lousy everyday way we have of trying to conceal our less-than-admirable motives.

"Sorry."

"It's okay." I climbed onto the bed and into a full-body cuddle. Unsure of how to justify my topic of early-morning conversation without admitting my arrogant intentions, I opted for avoidance.

This need to be right, to correct or blame others, is something I've carried with me for as long as I can remember. Years before, I might have criticized my husband outright, or seethed with a quiet fury and exploded weeks later without explanation. These days, the scene usually plays out more like the one above. Sometimes I might even see the mold and smile, remembering how grateful I am to be loved by this berry-gifting man.

Our brains so dutifully try to protect us. Mine warn me about the dangers of being wrong. I keep witnessing that, in reality, letting go brings me peace. My ongoing practice is to notice the pattern, shift my perspective, and make amends when necessary.

What imaginary dangers is your brain warning you about? Are you willing to practice shifting your mindset?

Perspective

What might help me create a more peaceful mindset?

- Ask myself, *How could this "bad" thing actually be a good thing?*
- Come up with a silly persona (a name and image) to represent the part of me that churns out fearful thoughts
- Remember someone who might be suffering more than I am
- When I notice a stressful thought, create some separation by mentally repeating, "I notice I'm having the thought that..."
- When upset with someone, imagine being in their shoes
- For 10 full minutes, imagine that I already have the future of my dreams
- Create/read a list of compliments I've received
- Look around me, find one beautiful thing, and notice every detail of its appearance
- Add laughter words to whatever I'm taking very seriously: *I was late to a meeting today... har-har. He's driving me crazy... lol. Life is meaningless... tee-hee.*
- Freewrite in a notebook without stopping to think, plan, or correct grammar

How else can I easily shift my perspective?

My favorite ideas

My favorite ways to take tender loving care of myself:

PART 2: COMMIT

GOALS AND REFLECTIONS

Tips

This section provides seven similar *Intention* sections so you can set self-care goals and reflect on the experience.

Write an effective goal by making it:

- Clear—you'll be able to look back and answer, *Did I do this?*
- Easy—you have no emotional resistance to doing it
- Meaningful—it's in the direction of something that truly matters to you

To more easily achieve your goal:

- Share it with someone
- Remind yourself regularly why it's important
- Reward yourself for progress and just because

What self-care means to me:

Why I am committed to my self-care:

Stuck

Not long ago, I was years into a project that felt like my most important work: writing a memoir about my experiences learning to thrive through depression. I had been getting up early and writing for thirty-plus minutes most mornings.

Then one day, without warning, I got stuck. Months went by without me writing or editing a single word.

As a trained life coach, I thought I knew what to do. I set my bar lower: I'd spend just fifteen minutes each morning on my book. Surely cutting my goal in half would make it easy? Yet for some reason, I still couldn't do it.

Then, upon a colleague's recommendation, I adjusted my goal to exactly two minutes. The next morning, I set a timer and stopped working after two minutes as she had advised. It was barely enough time to open my document and remember where I had left off the day before. But it worked. I kept at it for a couple of weeks, then gradually increased until I was back to regularly writing for thirty or more minutes.

I never figured out why I got stuck in the first place, and I didn't need to.

No matter what your goal, focus on the smallest next step— find a step so easy that you feel no emotional resistance to it. What matters isn't its size but that it's in the right direction and you take it.

All you ever have to take is one easy step.

Intention

Today's date:

Vision... What are my ideal self-care practices?

Focus... What is my most important goal?

Gut check... Is this goal: [ ] clear, [ ] easy, [ ] meaningful?
If not, how can I make it so?

Action... What's my next teeny-tiny step? (create a
calendar reminder, decide who to tell, treat myself for
filling out this page...)

Reflection

Today's date:

I'm grateful to myself for each step I've taken to care for
my own wellbeing, specifically:

Intention

Today's date:

Vision... What would exquisite self-care look like?

Focus... What one activity will I start, change, or stop to better care for me?

Gut check... Is this goal: [   ] clear, [   ] easy, [   ] meaningful? If not, what adjustments will I make?

Action... What's one easy-peasy action I'll take today to move forward? (write my goal on a bathroom mirror sticky note, text my goal to my BFF, take a nap...)

Reflection

Today's date:

There's no such thing as failure, only feedback.

Things that haven't gone so well and what each taught me:

Intention

Today's date:

Vision... In a few years when I'm living my ideal life, my self-care will look like this:

Focus... What's the one change I could make that would make everything else easier?

Gut check... Is this goal: [ ] clear, [ ] easy, [ ] meaningful?

Action... What can I do today to make progress? (put this book next to the coffeemaker, cut my goal in half, take my running shoes out of the closet...)

Reflection

Today's date:

10+ self-care wins I'm celebrating:

Intention

Today's date:

Vision... What are my ideal self-care practices?

Focus... What one activity will I start, change, or stop to improve my wellbeing?

Gut check... Is this goal: [ ] clear, [ ] easy, [ ] meaningful? If not, how can I make it so?

Action... What's my next teeny-tiny step?

Reflection

Today's date:

What has been effective for me in the past?

Some big self-care wins and how I achieved each one:

Intention

Today's date:

Vision... What would exquisite self-care look like?

Focus... What do I most want to improve next?

Gut check... Is this goal: [ ] clear, [ ] easy, [ ] meaningful?
If not, what adjustments will I make?

Action... What's one easy-peasy action I'll take today to
move forward?

Reflection

Today's date:

My favorite self-care wins:

_____

_____

_____

_____

_____

_____

_____

_____

_____

_____

_____

_____

_____

_____

_____

_____

_____

_____

Intention

Today's date:

Vision... In a few years when I'm living my ideal life, my self-care will look like this:

Focus... How do I most want to take better care of myself?

Gut check... Is this goal: [   ] clear, [   ] easy, [   ] meaningful?

Action... What can I do today to make progress?

Reflection

Today's date:

I deserve a round of applause. Here's why:

Intention

Today's date:

Vision... What are my ideal self-care practices?

Focus... What's my most important goal?

Gut check... Is this goal: [ ] clear, [ ] easy, [ ] meaningful?
If not, how can I make it so?

Action... What's my next teeny-tiny step?

Reflection

Today's date:

What I'm learning about myself through this self-care journey:

_____

_____

_____

_____

_____

_____

_____

_____

_____

_____

_____

_____

_____

_____

_____

_____

_____

PART 3: WRITE

JOURNALING PAGES

Tips

This section contains a series of journaling prompts followed by blank lined pages. Use these pages at any time to connect with your own creativity and wisdom about what you need. Consider adding newfound insights, activity ideas, and goals to the earlier sections of this book for quick reference.

The journaling prompts in the next pages relate to the following intentions:

- Snap out of it—Find calm in the midst of a stressful challenge
- Love myself—Feel love and gratitude toward yourself
- Think big—Refocus on what's most important to you
- Get unstuck—Find momentum when you're struggling to move forward
- Level up—Get new ideas, big and small, to improve your life
- Have fun—Brainstorm creative ideas for adventure
- Make a choice—Decide between options with clarity and confidence

You can answer the questions in order, flip to a random page, or skim through the pages for a prompt that aligns with your intention.

I find that my journaling is most effective, from getting new creative ideas to letting go of what's stressing me, when I write whatever comes to mind without pausing to plan or edit myself.

Snap out of it

What would I suggest to a friend with this problem?

Love myself

Dear Me,

I love you.

I love everything about you, even the bits that make you cringe. How could I not? There are nearly 8 billion people alive and, as Dr. Seuss says, not a single one of them is *Youer than You.*

I most especially appreciate these things about you:

_____

_____

_____

_____

_____

_____

_____

_____

_____

_____

Thanks for being you.

xo,

Me

Think big

What do I really want?

Get unstuck

What's the worst that can happen?

Level up

Who do I admire? What qualities do I admire in them?
Which of these qualities do I want to embody even more
than I already am?

Have fun

Professions I might have in an alternate life:

Make a choice

If I say Yes to this, what am I saying No to?

Snap out of it

What do I gain by hanging on to this struggle? What do I lose?

Love myself

I am grateful to myself for:

Think big

If I knew I had six months to live, how would I spend my time?

Get unstuck

How would Future Me handle this situation?

Level up

Who most needs my love today?

Have fun

Things I want to learn about:

Make a choice

My body is speaking to me. What is it saying?

Snap out of it

What three gifts can I find in this challenge?

Love myself

What makes me spontaneously smile?

_____

_____

_____

_____

_____

_____

_____

_____

_____

_____

_____

_____

_____

_____

_____

_____

_____

_____

_____

_____

Think big

Who am I?

Get unstuck

Where have I seen this challenge elsewhere in my life?

_____

_____

_____

_____

_____

_____

_____

_____

_____

_____

_____

_____

_____

_____

_____

_____

_____

_____

_____

_____

_____

Level up

What's draining my energy? (cluttered closet, overdue oil change, self-pressure, long work hours, bad relationship...)

What's one easy next step I could take to reduce one of these drainers and feel more energized?

Have fun

I'm going on a walking scavenger hunt and will look for these 5-10 items:

Make a choice

What is there to see about this decision that I'm not yet seeing?

Snap out of it

What do I need right now? How could I give myself 1% more of this?

_____

_____

_____

_____

_____

_____

_____

_____

_____

_____

_____

_____

_____

_____

_____

_____

Love myself

What does my mind, body, heart, and soul need to be well in this moment?

Think big

What's most important to me in life?

Get unstuck

What is it about this situation that I'm afraid to see?

Level up

How do I want to feel? What are some ways I could easily feel more of these emotions?

Have fun

Things I used to enjoy doing:

Make a choice

How could this be easy?

Snap out of it

How do I want to feel? Am I willing to feel this emotion?

Love myself

Things I love about myself:

Think big

Who do I want to be?

Get unstuck

What is it about this situation that's most important to me?

_____

_____

_____

_____

_____

_____

_____

_____

_____

_____

_____

_____

_____

_____

_____

_____

_____

Level up

What do I need to know today?

Have fun

Hobbies that sound interesting:

Make a choice

What would feel like play?

Snap out of it

What am I making this mean?

Love myself

What I've learned about self-care:

Think big

What would I do if I knew I couldn't fail?

Get unstuck

Am I willing to move forward? Why or why not?

Level up

What do I complain about to others or myself? How could I
eliminate each of these complaints?

Have fun

Silly things I might like to try once:

Make a choice

What's the one thing I could do that would make everything else easier?

Snap out of it

What would Future Me say about this situation?

Love myself

What would feel like love right now?

_____

_____

_____

_____

_____

_____

_____

_____

_____

_____

_____

_____

_____

_____

_____

_____

_____

_____

_____

_____

_____

_____

_____

Think big

How can I serve today?

Get unstuck

What are some more effective questions I could ask myself?

_____

_____

_____

_____

_____

_____

_____

_____

_____

_____

_____

_____

_____

_____

_____

_____

_____

_____

_____

_____

_____

_____

Level up

If there were no constraints on my time, money, or energy, what would I love to have, do, and be?

Have fun

Skills that would be cool to have:

Make a choice

Which option feels the most like freedom?

Snap out of it

What's the real challenge here for me?

CLOSING

Cluttered

Do you ever feel cluttered inside?

I perfected the skill of packing away my feelings at an early age. At seven, I was afraid to further upset my family after my mom's sudden death. By adulthood, I was scared of being seen as the most fragile team member in the room. I used stiff, opaque bins of logic-defying denial stacked next to cardboard boxes that bowed under the pressure of outrage. Duct tape layered over mourning and double-wrapped over perceived abandonment.

By my late twenties, I was bedbound by a recurrence of depression. Out of options, I began to unshelve those bins and peel away their protective strips. I wondered how long it would take to clear the clutter. Other people seemed to have such easy access to happiness.

Would I ever be happy like them?

Now, with ample therapy, coaching, and another decade of life itself under my belt, I experience only glimpses of the hopelessness that used to consume me. But it's not as easy as I'd once hoped. My goal has shifted from *feeling better* to *getting better at feeling*—which requires consistent tender loving self-care.

I no longer think we're meant to realize some satisfying Marie Kondō tidied-up ideal, a decluttering of the emotional self that can be checked off of a to-do list. I think being among the clutter might be what makes life so much fun.

I wish for you a little more peace, a little more joy, and endless self-compassion.

Thank you.

About the author

Mandy Kubicek is a Certified Life Coach who specializes in helping high-achieving women build careers they love.

Before training with Martha Beck (aka Oprah's life coach), Mandy spent twelve years overachieving in the software industry. She has an MBA from Washington University in St. Louis, a BS from the University of Nebraska–Lincoln, and is a lifelong learner.

Known for her insightful questions and giant salads, Mandy lives in downtown Omaha, Nebraska, with her husband and boxer-coonhound.

Visit www.coachkubicek.com for free digital resources to help you love your work.

CPSIA information can be obtained
at www.ICGtesting.com
Printed in the USA
LVHW051032250121
677406LV00006B/498